The Fajita Cookbook Must Have

Classic to Modern and Flavorful Fajita Recipes

By: Logan King

Copyright © 2022 by Logan King

Edition Notice

The author has taken any step to make sure this book is accurate and safe. Every info is checked. However, every step you take following the book do it with caution and on your own accord.

If you end up with a copied and illegal version of this book please delete it and get the original. This will support the author to create even better books for everyone. Also, if possible report where you have found the illegal version.

Table of Contents

Introduction

All the credits for the invention of our tasty Fajitas go to the Mexican Ranch Workers. Those workers used to live in west Texas along with the border of Mexico-Texas. In the early 1940s, a steer was butchered, and the workers were given a chance to have the desired parts in exchange for their partial wages. Due to this, the workers learned how to use tough-cut beef, commonly known as Skirt Steak.

In Spanish, the work Fajita is derived from the word fava that refers to belt or griddle in English. The truth is that fajita is a recipe that truly is a combination of Tex-Mex food. It is a blend of Texas Cowboys and Mexican Ranchero foods. In recent times, the fajita has lost its real meaning and is used to describe anything that has been cooked and served rolled up in a flour tortilla. But well, who doesn't love fajitas and this book is a gift for you.

Recipe 1 - Backed Chicken Fajitas:

This recipe is one of the fantastic fajita recipes cooked quickly and liberally served with hot sauce.

Serving Size: 6 servings

Total Time: 45 minutes

Ingredients:

- 1 lb. boneless and skinless chicken breasts chopped into strips
- 14-1/2 ounces can of diced tomatoes
- 14-1/2 ounces can of green chilies
- 2 tablespoons Chili powder
- 1 medium onion
- 2 Sliced green peppers
- 2 Sliced sweet red peppers
- 2 tablespoons Canola oil
- 2 tablespoons ground cumin
- ¼ teaspoons Salt
- 12 Warmed flour tortillas
- Sliced avocados, tomatoes, and lime wedges as you like

Instructions:

Prepare a baking dish by coating it with cooking spray.

Using a medium-sized bowl, combine tomatoes, onion, green chilies, and peppers.

In another bowl, mix salt, cumin powder, chili powder, and oil.

Shift the prepared mixture into the chicken and toss to coat properly.

Remove cover and start baking at 400°, taking 25-30 minutes.

Continue cooking until the chicken is no longer pink.

With the help of a spoon, place the chicken mixture over the tortillas.

Fold tortillas and serve hit with toppings as desired.

Recipe 2 - Southwest Fajita Wraps:

This recipe is an incredible way to use beef in making delicious and juicy fajita wraps.

Serving Size: 8 servings

Total Time: 3 hours 20 minutes

Ingredients:

- 1-1/2 lb. sirloin steaks beef
- 2 tablespoons Canola oil
- 1-1/2 teaspoons Crushed red pepper flakes
- 2 tablespoons Lemon juice
- 1 minced garlic clove
- 1-1/2 teaspoons ground cumin
- 1 teaspoon Seasoned salt
- ½ teaspoon Chili powder
- 1 large-sized sweet red pepper
- 1 large-sized onion
- 8 Mini flour tortillas
- Shredded Cheddar cheese as you like
- Fresh Cilantro leaves as you like
- Sliced Jalapeno peppers as you like
- Avocados as you like

Instructions:

Using a large-sized skillet, add oil and heat over medium flame.

Place steak and the dipping into a slow cooker, then add lemon, cumin, salt, garlic, red pepper, and chili powder.

Cover up and cook on a high heat flame. Continue cooking until the meat turns out to be tender, taking 2 hours.

Add onions and red pepper to the skillet. Cover up and start cooking for an hour until the meat and vegetables are tender.

Heat up the tortillas as per the package directions.

With the help of a spoon, place some cooked beef and vegetables in the center. Top up as desired.

Recipe 3 - Flavorful Fajita Recipe:

This recipe is a delicious and amazing with a finger-licking good taste.

Serving Size: 6 servings

Total Time: 30 minutes

Ingredients:

- 4 tablespoons Canola oil
- 1 teaspoon Garlic powder
- ½ teaspoon Paprika
- ½ teaspoon red pepper flakes crushed, optional
- 1½ teaspoons dried oregano
- 1-1/2 lbs. Boneless and skinless chicken breasts
- 1/2 teaspoon Chili powder
- A half medium-sized sweet red pepper
- 1½ teaspoons seasoned salt
- A half medium-sized green pepper
- 4 thinly sliced green onions
- ½ teaspoons cumin ground
- ½ cup Chopped onion
- 2 tablespoons Lemon juice
- 6 warmed flour tortillas

Optional:

- Shredded cheddar cheese
- Taco sauce
- Salsa
- Guacamole
- Sliced red onions
- Sour cream

Instructions:

Combine lemon juice, seasonings, and 2 tbsp. oil in a big bowl; add chicken to the mixture.

Toss to coat.

Cover up and refrigerate it for 1 to 4 hours.

Either a large-sized cast-iron skillet, add onions and peppers and wait until sauté in the rest of the oil to make it crisp-tender.

Remove from the skillet, and then keep warm.

Drain the chicken and discard the marinade.

Use this skillet and cook chicken on medium-high heat, taking 5-6 minutes and until not pink any longer.

Return this mixture of pepper to the pan and heat thoroughly.

With the help of a spoon, place down, filling the middle of tortillas, then fold in half.

Serve with toppings as desired.

Recipe 4 - Squash Fajita with Goat Cheese:

This recipe is an amazing way to cook fajitas with a topping of goat cheese.

Serving Size: 4 servings

Total Time: 30 minutes

Ingredients:

- 2 lbs. Sliced yellow summer squash
- 1 sweet onion finely chopped
- 2 tablespoons Olive oil
- 4 minced garlic cloves
- 1 teaspoon Pepper
- 1/2 teaspoon salt
- 8 Flour tortillas
- 4 ounces fresh goat cheese crumbled
- 2 tablespoons freshly minced parsley

Instructions:

Using a large-sized skillet, sauté squash and onion in oil until it turns out to be tender.

Add in pepper, salt, and garlic; cook a minute longer.

With the help of a spoon, shift the mixture onto the warmed tortillas.

Top up with some cheese and sprinkle with some parsley.

Fold in sides.

Recipe 5 - Steak Fajitas:

This recipe is an amazing way to enjoy a steak with the flavors of fajita.

Serving Size: 6 servings

Total Time: 30 minutes

Ingredients:

- 2 large-seeded and chopped tomatoes
- 1/2 cup diced red onion
- 1/4 cup Lime juice
- 1 seeded and minced jalapeno pepper
- 3 tablespoons minced fresh cilantro
- 1 tablespoon Canola oil
- 2 teaspoons ground cumin
- 3/4 teaspoon salt
- 1-1/2 lbs. beef flank steak
- A halved and sliced large onion
- 6 Warmed whole wheat tortillas
- Sliced avocado
- Lime wedges

Instructions:

For the preparation of salsa, start by combining seeded tomatoes, onions, jalapeno peppers, lime juice, and cilantro in a small-sizes bowl.

Stir in a teaspoon of salt and cumin.

Let the mixture sit until serving.

Sprinkle the remaining salt and cumin over the steak.

Cover up and grill the steak over medium heat flame or broil from heat until meat reaches desired doneness to get it done at medium-rare. A thermometer should read 135° taking 6-8 minutes.

Let it stand for at least 5 minutes.

In the meantime, with the help of a skillet, add oil and heat over medium-high heat flame.

Add onions and continue cooking until sautéed and it becomes crisp-tender.

Chop down the steak into thin slices across the grain.

Serve the steak in tortillas topped up with the prepared salsa and sautéed onions.

If desired, serve with some additional toppings of lime wedges and avocados to enhance the flavors.

Recipe 6 - Fajita in a bowl:

The fajitas can be eaten in many ways, but most people prefer is having it in tortillas.

Serving Size: 4 servings

Total Time: 30 minutes

Ingredients:

- A beef flank steak of 1 lb.
- 1 tablespoon Brown sugar
- ½ teaspoon salt
- ½ cup Reduced-fat lime vinaigrette
- 1 tablespoon Chili powder
- A dozen halved and seeded sweet peppers miniature
- 2 cups Cherry tomatoes
- 1 medium-sized red onion (thin wedges)
- 1 cup cilantro leaves fresh
- A pair of sweet corn medium ears with husks removed
- 12 cups mixed Torn salad greens

Optional:

- Cottage cheese
- Tortillas
- Lime wedges

Instructions:

Using a small-sized bowl, prepare a mixture of chili powder, salt, and brown sugar.

Rub it onto both sides on the steak piece properly that the spices get deeply into it.

Once the marinating is done, place onions and peppers on a grilling grid.

Place it on grill rack on medium heat flame. Cover up and grill until it turns out to be crisp-tender by stirring it occasionally, taking at least 9-11 minutes.

Add in tomatoes right in the last two minutes, then remove from the grill.

Place the corn and steak directly on the grill rack and cover it up by closing the lid.

Grill the steak, taking 8 to 10 minutes from each side.

Keep on grilling the corn until it's lightly charred by sporadically turning for 10 to 12 minutes.

Divide the cilantro and greens among 4 separate bowls.

Cut the corn from its cobs and slice the steak thinly across the grain.

Place the steak pieces in bowls.

Top up with some vegetables.

Drizzle with some vinaigrette.

If desired, you can serve with some additional toppings of tortillas, lime, and cheese.

Recipe 7 - Skillet Chicken Fajitas:

This recipe is a love for all the people that like to have fresh flavors with a twist of Fajitas.

Serving Size: 6 servings

Total Time: 30 minutes

Ingredients:

- 1/4 cup Lime juice
- A minced garlic cloves
- 1 teaspoon Chili powder
- 1/2 teaspoon salt
- 1/2 teaspoon ground cumin
- 1/2 medium yellow pepper chopped into strips
- 2 tablespoons olive oil
- 1-1/2 lbs. Boneless skinless chicken breasts, cut into strips
- 1 medium onion chopped into thin wedges
- ½ medium sweet red pepper chopped into strips
- 1/2 cup Salsa
- 12 warmed flour tortillas
- 1/2 medium green pepper, cut into strips
- 1-1/2 cups shredded cheddar cheese or Monterey Jack cheese

Instructions:

Start by combining the ground cumin, salt, chili powder, minced garlic, and lime juice.

Add a tablespoon of oil to the dry spices.

Add chicken to the marinating and start tossing to coat until properly coated.

Let the chicken sit in the stand, marinated for 15 minutes.

Using a large-sized nonstick skillet, heat the remaining oil over medium-high heat flame.

Add onions and wait until sauté.

Add peppers to the skillet and continue cooking until crisp-tender taking 3-4 minutes.

Remove from pan.

Using the same skillet, add the prepared chicken mixture and cook well until sauté, or it turns out to be no longer pink, taking 3-4 minutes. Add in salsa and pepper mixture and keep on stirring.

Heat thoroughly.

With the help of a spoon, place cooked chicken in tortillas.

Sprinkle with some additional cheese.

Recipe 8 - Fajita Burger Wraps:

The fajita burger wrap is a combination of tender meat and crunchy veggies.

Serving Size: 4 servings

Total Time: 30 minutes

Ingredients:

- 2 teaspoons canola oil
- 1 lb. ground beef 90% lean
- 1 medium-sized green pepper, chopped into thin strips
- 2 tablespoons seasoning mix fajita
- 1 medium-sized onion sliced
- 1 red sweet pepper medium chopped into thinly sized strips
- 4 Flour tortillas
- ¾ cup cheddar cheese Shredded

Instructions:

Using a large-sized bowl, combine both the seasoning mix and beef; continue mixing with light hands but properly.

Shape it into four thick patties.

Using a large-sized skillet, add oil and heat on medium heat flame.

Add the burgers cook for 4 minutes from each side.

Remove it from the pan.

In the same skillet, you will add peppers and onions to the skillet.

Continue cooking and stirring for 5 to 7 minutes and until tender and lightly browned.

With the help of a spoon, place the mixture in the middle of every tortilla, and then place the pepper mixture, a burger, along 3 tbsp. full of cheese.

Fold the sides of the tortilla over the burger.

Make a square by folding the bottom and top to close. Wipe the skillet clean.

Place the wraps with the seam side facing down and cook in the skillet for 1 to 2 minutes from every side until golden.

Recipe 9 - Busy Day Chicken Fajitas:

This recipe is a very easy and convenient way to enjoy fajitas in a very short time.

Serving Size: 6 servings

Total Time: 4 hours and 20 minutes

Ingredients:

- 1 lb. Boneless skinless chicken breasts
- 1 medium-sized green pepper chopped into strips
- ½ teaspoon ground cumin
- 1 large-sized onion sliced
- 1-1/2 cups picante sauce
- ½ teaspoon garlic powder
- 1 can (15 ounces) Rinsed and drained black beans
- 12 Warmed flour tortillas
- 2 cups shredded cheddar cheese
- 2 thinly sliced green onions

Optional:

- Chopped tomatoes
- Sour cream

Instructions:

Start by placing the chicken in a slow cooker.

Add onions, pepper, and black beans.

Using a small-sized bowl, mix cumin, garlic powder, and picante sauce.

Pour the mixture over the top.

Cover up and start cooking on low heat flame until the chicken is tender, taking at least 4-5 hours.

Remove the cooked chicken, let it sit aside, and cool slightly.

With the help of 2 forks, start to shred the chicken and return to the slow cooker.

Heat it thoroughly.

Serve hot with tortillas topped up with cheese, onions and the toppings of your choice.

Recipe 10 - Simple Grilled Steak Fajitas:

This recipe is an effortless fajita recipe that makes it lovely to enjoy steak fajita at home.

Serving Size: 4 servings

Total Time: 30 minutes

Ingredients:

- 1 lb. Sirloin steak beef top
- 1 medium-sized halved into two pieces sweet red pepper
- 1 medium-sized halved into two pieces green pepper
- 2 tablespoons fajita seasoning
- 1 tablespoon olive oil
- 1 large-sized sweet onion chopped into crosswise slices
- 4 warmed tortillas whole wheat

Optional:

- Sliced avocado
- Fresh cilantro minced
- Lime wedges

Instructions:

Start by rubbing the steak using seasoning mix and brush peppers and onion with oil.

Cover up and grill the vegetables and steak on the greased rack on medium heat for at least 4 to 6 minutes from each side and until the meat becomes desired doneness.

Make the steak medium-rare, and then remove it from the grill when vegetables become tender.

Let the steak stand for 5 minutes covered just before slicing.

Cut steak and vegetables into strips.

Serve them in tortillas.

If desired you can top with some cilantro and avocado.

Recipe 11 - Fajita in Pitas:

This recipe is one of the easiest and affordable recipes to make at home. You can enjoy it with your family.

Serving Size: 4 serving

Total Time: 25 min

Ingredients:

- ½ cup mayonnaise
- 8 lettuce leaves
- 1 chopped green onion
- 4 teaspoons dijon mustard
- Boneless and skinless chicken breast halves 3 of 6 ounces each
- 2 halved, seeded medium sweet red peppers
- 1/4 teaspoon pepper
- 2 halved, seeded green peppers medium
- 8 warmed pita pocket halves

Instructions:

Mix peppers, mustard, green onion, and mayonnaise in a bowl and reserve just 1/3 cup to assemble.

Spread the remaining mixture on peppers and chicken.

Grill peppers and chicken covered on medium heat for 6 minutes from each side.

Cut the chicken into slices of ½ inch and peppers into slices of 1 inch.

Spread the reserved mixture inside the pita and fill using peppers, chicken, and lettuce.

Recipe 12 - Veggie Fajitas:

It is one the most eating dish and favorite of all ones who like to eat and enjoy the real taste.

Serving Size: 8 servings

Total Time: 25 minutes

Ingredients:

- A small-sized zucchini thinly sliced
- A medium-sized yellow summer squash thinly sliced
- 1 cup salsa
- 1/2 lb. sliced fresh mushrooms
- A small-sized onion halved and sliced
- A medium-sized carrot julienned
- 1 teaspoon salt
- 1/2 teaspoon pepper
- 1 tablespoon canola oil
- 1 cup sour cream
- 8 warmed flour tortillas
- 2 cups shredded cheddar cheese

Instructions:

Using large-sized cast-iron or other heavy skillets. Add some oil and cook vegetables with salt and pepper in oil until crisp-tender taking 5-7 minutes.

With the help of a slotted spoon, place about 1/2 cup of the vegetable mixture in the center of each tortilla.

Sprinkle each tortilla with 1/4 cup of cheese.

Top up with sour cream and salsa.

Fold in sides.

Recipe 13 – Portobello Fajitas

This recipe is one of the amazing Portobello fajitas recipes cooked in a short time served with hot sauce.

Serving size: 4 servings

Total time: 30 minutes

Ingredients:

- 3 portobello mushrooms Large
- 2 tablespoons lime juice
- 1 sweet red pepper Large, cut into thin strips
- A half large sweet onion sliced
- 4 flour tortillas of 8 inches warmed
- 1/2 cup cheddar cheese shredded
- A half-cup salad dressing Italian
- Optional toppings: guacamole, salsa, and sour cream

Instructions:

Remove the stems of the mushroom and discard using a spoon. Scrape, remove the gills.

Cut mushrooms into slices of ½ inch and place in the bowl.

Add onion and pepper and drizzle using salad dressing. Toss well to coat.

Let the mixture stand for 10 minutes and transfer the vegetables to the open grill or grill wok.

Grill for 10 minutes covered on medium heat and until tender while stirring occasionally

Drizzle using lime juice and serve with toppings, cheese, and tortillas.

Recipe 14 - Sausage Fajitas

This recipe is one of the delicious sausage fajitas recipes cooked in a short time served with hot sauce.

Serving size: 4 servings

Total time: 35 minutes

Ingredients:

- 1 cup chicken broth reduced sodium
- 1/4 cup olive oil
- 3 cups sweet peppers julienned mixed
- 1/4 cup soy sauce reduced-sodium
- 1 tablespoon each oregano, dried basil, and thyme
- 1/4 teaspoon pepper
- 1 medium thinly sliced red onion
- 1 small tomato, chopped
- 1 cup mushrooms sliced fresh
- 3/4 lb. smoked turkey kielbasa, sliced
- 1/4 cup Worcestershire sauce
- 4 tortillas whole wheat (8 inches) warmed
- 1/4 cup wine vinegar red
- 4 tablespoons sour cream fat-free

Instructions:

Combine pepper, herbs, Worcestershire sauce, soy sauce, vinegar, oil, and broth in a plastic bag.

Add mushrooms, onion, peppers, and sausage and seal the bag. Refrigerate for 2 hours.

Drain the marinade but reserve ½ cup. Cook vegetables and sausage in a skillet with set aside marinade for 10 minutes.

Spoon the mixture of sausage on each tortilla with tomato and sour cream.

Recipe 15 - Beef Fajita

This recipe is one of the delightful beef fajitas recipes cooked in a short time served with hot sauce.

Serving size: 2 servings

Total time: 35 minutes

Ingredients:

- ¼ cup vegetable oil
- 3 green onions, thinly sliced
- 3 garlic cloves, minced
- ¼ cup lemon juice
- 1-1/2 teaspoons grated lemon zest
- 1/4 teaspoon pepper
- 1 flank steak beef (about ¾ lb.) cut into strips
- ¼- ½ teaspoon chili powder
- 4 flour tortillas of 8 inches
- Salsa, optional

Instructions:

Combine meat, pepper, chili powder, lemon zest, garlic, lemon juice and oil in a bowl and place in the refrigerator. Refrigerate for four to eight hours.

Discard the marinade after draining. Heat reserved marinade in the skillet and add green onions and meat.

Cook while stirring until the meat is done. Place meat mixture ½ cup in the middle of every tortilla with a slotted spoon.

Top using salsa if you like and fold the sides over the mixture of meat.

Recipe 16 - Pork fajitas

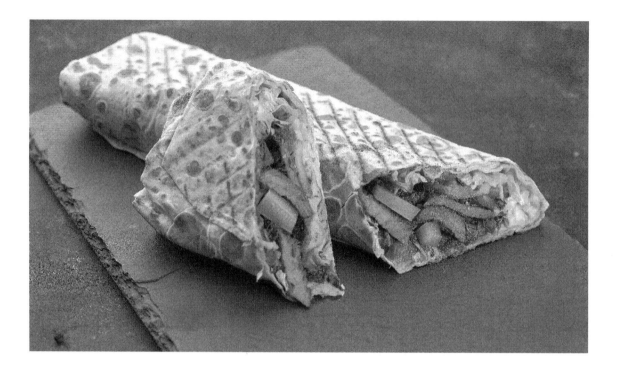

This recipe is one of the lovely pork fajita recipes cooked in a short time served with hot sauce.

Serving size: 6 servings

Total time: 25 minutes

Ingredients:

- 1 lb. boneless pork
- 1 medium julienned green pepper
- 1 teaspoon ground cumin
- 1/2 teaspoon hot pepper sauce
- 2 garlic cloves, minced
- 2 tablespoons vinegar
- 1 teaspoon dried oregano
- 2 tablespoons orange juice
- ½ teaspoon seasoned salt
- 1 medium onion, cut into wedges
- 6 flour tortillas of 6 inches
- 1 tablespoon vegetable oil
- shredded lettuce, salsa, dried tomatoes, or sour cream are optional

Instructions:

Cut pork into small strips and set aside. In the plastic bag, combine pepper sauce, salt, cumin, oregano, garlic, vinegar, and orange juice and mix well.

Add the pork and close the bag. Chill for an hour.

Cook marinade with pork on medium heat in a skillet along with green pepper and onion in oil until the vegetables become tender and pork is not pink any longer.

Place filling ¾ cup in the middle of every tortilla and top with optional toppings if you like.

Fold in tortilla sides and serve instantly.

Recipe 17 – Venison Fajitas

This recipe is one of the wonderful venison fajitas recipes cooked in a short time served with hot sauce.

Serving size: 4 servings

Total time: 25 minutes

Ingredients:

- ½ cup orange juice
- ¼ teaspoon cayenne pepper
- 1 tablespoon salt
- 1 ½ lb. venison/ flank steak elk, cut into strips
- 2 tablespoons vegetable oil
- ¼ cup white vinegar
- 1 green pepper medium julienned
- ¼ teaspoon pepper
- Sour cream, salsa optional
- 1 onion medium, halved, sliced
- 8 flour tortillas of 8 inches
- 1 sweet red pepper medium, julienned
- 2 cups Mexican cheese shredded blend/ cheddar cheese

Instructions:

Combine white vinegar, orange juice, salt, pepper, and cayenne pepper and meat in the plastic bag. Seal it and refrigerate for about 2 hours after turning to coat.

Discard the marinade after draining. Sauté onion and pepper in oil 1 tbsp until tender yet crisp. Set aside.

Heat the rest of the oil and stir fry the meat for 5 minutes. Return the vegetables to this pan and heat through.

Spoon the meat mixture on tortillas. Top using sour cream and cheese if you like.

Fold in tortilla sides.

Recipe 18 - Fajita Frittata

This recipe is one of the pleasant Frittata fajita recipes cooked in a short time and provides an excellent flavor.

Serving size: 8 servings

Total time: 25 minutes

Ingredients:

- ½ lb. boneless and skinless chicken breast, cut into strips
- 1 onion small, cut into small strips
- ½ green pepper medium, cut into strips
- 1 teaspoon lime juice
- ½ teaspoon ground cumin
- 2 cups egg substitute
- 2 tablespoons canola oil
- ½ teaspoon chili powder
- ½ teaspoon salt
- 1 cup Colby -Monterey Jack shredded cheese
- Salsa, sour cream, optional

Instructions:

In a large ovenproof skillet, sauté the chicken, onion, green pepper, lime juice, salt, cumin, and chili powder in oil until chicken is no longer pink.

Pour egg substitute over chicken mixture. Cover and cook over medium-low heat for 8-10 minutes or until nearly set.

Uncover; broil 6 in. from the heat for 2-3 minutes or until eggs are set.

Sprinkle with cheese. Cover and let stand for 1-minute or until cheese is melted.

Serve with salsa and sour cream if desired.

Recipe 19 - Hearty Fajitas

This recipe is one of the enjoyable hearty fajita recipes that get ready quickly and makes a hearty meal.

Serving size: 14 servings

Total time: 30 minutes

Ingredients:

- 2 tablespoons canola oil
- ½ lb. medium uncooked shrimp, peeled, deveined
- 1 teaspoon salt
- ½ lb. beef boneless top round steak, cut into small strips
- 1 green pepper medium, thinly sliced
- 2 tomatoes medium, cut into small wedges
- 1 sweet red pepper medium, thinly sliced
- 1 can of 16 ounces refried beans
- 2 onions small, thinly sliced
- 2 teaspoons chili powder
- ½ cup part-skim shredded mozzarella cheese
- 1/4 lb. boneless and skinless chicken breast, cut into small strips
- 14 warmed flour tortillas of 8 inches

Instructions:

Stir fry the chicken and steak in a skillet using oil. Add salt, chili powder, tomatoes, onions, peppers, and shrimp and cook until the vegetables become crisp-tender and meat juices are clear.

Cook cheese and refried beans in a saucepan until the cheese melts.

Spoon this mixture on tortillas and top using meat mixture.

Recipe 20 - Fajitas Skillet

This recipe is one of the delicious skillet fajita recipes that you make in a skillet.

Serving size: 4 servings

Total time: 30 minutes

Ingredients:

- 3 tablespoons divided olive oil
- 1 teaspoon cornstarch
- ½ lb. boneless skinless chicken breasts, cut into strips
- 2 teaspoons brown sugar
- ½ lb. beef top sirloin steak, cut into thin strips
- 1 onion small, sliced
- ½ teaspoon chili powder
- 2 flour tortillas of 10 inches, cut into strips of 1/2-inch
- ¼ teaspoon pepper
- 1 green pepper medium, sliced
- 2 tablespoons soy sauce
- 2 teaspoons lime juice
- ½ teaspoon ground cumin
- 1 cup fresh cubed pineapple
- 1 tomato medium, coarsely chopped

Instructions:

In a large skillet, fry tortilla strips in 2 tablespoons oil on both sides for 1-minute or until golden brown. Drain on paper towels.

In the same skillet, cook the chicken, beef, green pepper, onion, soy sauce, brown sugar, chili powder, cumin, and pepper in the remaining oil for 3-4 minutes or until chicken is no longer pink.

In a small bowl, combine corn starch and lime juice until smooth; add to the pan.

Bring to a boil; cook and stir for a minute or until thickened.

Stir in pineapple and tomato; heat through. Serve with tortilla strips.

Recipe 21 - Shrimp Fajitas

Who doesn't love shrimp fajitas that can be made with such ease at home? Try it now.

Serving size: 4 servings

Total time: 30 minutes

Ingredients:

- 1 lb. uncooked shrimp medium, peeled, deveined
- 1 tablespoon and 2 teaspoons divided olive oil
- 1/8 teaspoon ground cumin
- 1 cup sour cream fat-free
- 4 tablespoons fresh divided cilantro minced
- 3 teaspoons Caribbean jerk seasoning
- 1 onion large, halved, thinly sliced
- 1/8 teaspoon chili powder
- 1 sweet red pepper medium, cut into small strips
- 8 warmed flour tortillas of 6 inches
- 1 green pepper medium, cut into small strips
- ½ cup salsa

Instructions:

Toss shrimp with spices, oil 1 tbsp, cilantro 2 tsp in a bowl. Let the mixture stand for 10 minutes.

Mix remaining cilantro and sour cream in the small bowl.

Coat a nonstick skillet using cooking spray and heat oil 1 tsp on medium heat.

Add peppers and onion and cook while stirring until they are crisp-tender. Now remove from the pan.

Heat the remaining oil on medium heat in this pan and add the shrimp. Cook while stirring until shrimp becomes pink.

Add the onion mixture to this pan and heat through.

Serve with sour cream mixture, salsa, and tortillas.

Recipe 22 - Turkey Fajitas

This recipe is one of the delicious Turkey fajitas recipes that are loved by all.

Serving size: 4 servings

Total time: 30 minutes

Ingredients:

- 1 tablespoon canola oil
- 1 lb. boneless turkey tenderloins breast cut into strips
- 1 each red, green, sweet, yellow pepper medium, cut into strips of 1/4-inch
- 1 onion medium, thinly sliced
- 1 minced garlic clove
- ½ teaspoon salt
- ½ teaspoon ground cumin
- ½ teaspoon pepper
- ¼ teaspoon cayenne pepper
- ½ cup minced fresh cilantro
- ¼ cup lime juice
- 8 warmed flour tortillas of 6 inches

Instructions:

In a large nonstick skillet, heat oil over medium-high heat. Next, add turkey cook and stir for 2 minutes.

Add peppers, onion, garlic, salt, cumin, pepper, and cayenne.

Cook and stir 5 minutes or until turkey is no longer pink and pepper is crisp-tender.

Stir in cilantro and lime juice cook 1 minute longer. Serve in tortillas.

Recipe 23 - Fajitas Potato Skins

This recipe is one of the delightful fajita potato skins recipes cooked in a short time served with hot sauce.

Serving size: 4 servings

Total time: 20 minutes

Ingredients:

- 8 russet potatoes small-medium, washed, dried
- ½ cup green pepper chopped
- Salt, pepper to taste
- 2 tablespoons divided canola oil
- 1 chicken breast large
- ½ cup yellow pepper chopped
- 3 tablespoons melted unsalted butter
- 4 teaspoons taco seasoning McCormick Gluten-Free, divided
- ½ cup red pepper chopped
- 1½ cup cheddar cheese freshly grated
- 4 green onions chopped
- Salsa, sour cream, for topping
- ½ cup onion chopped

Instructions:

Preheat the oven to about 400 F.

Pierce every potato using a knife multiple times and place the potatoes on the rack of the oven for 45 to 50 minutes and until they are fork-tender.

Remove potatoes from the oven. Allow them to cool for 10 to 15 minutes.

Cut these potatoes lengthwise in half and use a spoon for scooping out their flesh. Just leave ¼ inches intact. Now set your oven to broiling.

Put potatoes with skin side up on the baking sheet and brush each using melted butter.

Turn these potatoes over. Brush again using melted butter. Season every potato with pepper and salt.

Flip and broil for a minute with the skin side facing up. Using tongs, flip, and broil again.

Remove from the oven and sprinkle cheese on each potato.

Top using fajita chicken mixture and some more cheese.

Broil potatoes in the broiler for 2 to 3 minutes.

For making Chicken Fajita Stuffing:

Warm the 1 tablespoon of oil in a skillet over medium

Season each side of the chicken breast with 1 teaspoon of taco seasoning and a generous pinch of salt and pepper

The chicken within the warm Cook dinner on each facet for six-7 minutes, or until the inner temperature reaches 160 levels F.

Dispose of the skillet from the pan and flip the warmth right down to medium-low.

Add last, oil to the pan. Once the oil is heated, upload the chopped peppers and onions. Sprinkle with a beneficent pinch of salt and add the final 2 teaspoons of taco seasoning prepare dinner, stirring now and again, until the peppers are smooth about 5

Whilst the peppers are cooking, chop the chicken into small

Take the pan off the heat and stir within the chopped chicken. Season the aggregate with salt and pepper to taste.

Recipe 24 - Pepper Pork Fajitas

Enjoy these delicious Pepper Pork Fajitas recipes, which will make your day.

Serving size: 6 servings

Total time: 35 minutes

Ingredients:

- ½ teaspoon chili chipotle powder
- 1 tablespoon paprika
- 2 bell peppers red, cut into strips of 1-inch
- 1 teaspoon ground cumin
- ½ teaspoon garlic powder
- 2 teaspoons brown sugar
- salt to taste
- 1 ½ teaspoons chili powder
- 1 tablespoon olive oil
- Juice of a lime and more as needed
- 2 bell peppers yellow, cut into strips of 1-inch
- 2 red onions large, thickly sliced
- 1½ lbs. boneless center-cut 1-inch-thick pork chops
- 3 tablespoons olive oil, and more to oil grill grates

Instructions:

Mix salt 1 tsp, garlic powder, chipotle chili powder, cumin, chili powder, brown sugar, and paprika in a bowl.

Toss pork chops with lime juice and oil in the container and rub using spice mixture.

Refrigerate covered for about 2 hours.

Heat a skillet cast-iron on medium heat. Toss the onions and peppers in the bowl along with salt 1 tsp, lime juice, and oil.

Add the mixture of onion pepper into the skillet. Cook while stirring occasionally for 8 minutes or so and set aside.

On medium heat, prepare your outdoor grill and brush the grill grates lightly. Grill the chops for 4 minutes from each side.

Transfer it to the cutting board and let it rest for about 10 minutes and slice it thinly.

Serve it with sour cream, chopped scallions, salsa, pepper jack cheese, lime wedges, pickled jalapenos, guacamole, and onions.

Recipe 25 - Warm Fajita Salad

Try this tasty warm fajita salad recipe and savor the salad taste for a long time to come.

Serving size: 6 serving

Total time: 30 minutes

Ingredients:

- 1 teaspoon dried oregano
- ½ cup lime juice
- 1 teaspoon ground cumin
- 1 lb. skinless boneless chicken breasts, cut into small strips
- 4 tablespoons divided canola oil
- 1 onion medium, cut into wedges
- 2 minced garlic cloves
- 1 sweet red pepper medium, cut into strips
- 1 cup toasted unbalanced almonds
- 2 cans of 4 ounces each green chilies chopped
- 3 cups lettuce shredded
- 1 ripe avocado medium, peeled, sliced
- 3 tomatoes medium, cut into small wedges

Instructions:

In a bowl, combine 2 tbsp oil, garlic, cumin, lime juice, and oregano.

Pour half in a large bowl or dish, add chicken and turn to coat.

Marinate for at least 30 minutes. Cover and refrigerate the remaining marinade.

In a large skillet, heat remaining oil on medium-high. Sauté onion for 2-3 minutes or until crisp-tender.

Drain chicken, discarding marinade. Add chicken to skillet stir-fry until meat is no longer pink.

Add the red pepper, chilies, and reserved marinade cook 2 minutes or until heated through. Stir in almonds.

Serve immediately over shredded lettuce top with tomatoes and avocado.

Recipe 26 - Pork Fajita kabobs:

This recipe is one of the wonderful pork fajitas kabobs recipes that are as delicious as they look.

Serving size: 6 servings

Total time: 30 minutes

Ingredients:

- 1 lb. boneless all natural trimmed, Smithfield Loin Filet, cut into pieces of 1 inch
- 1 teaspoon cumin
- 1 bell pepper orange, cut into pieces of 1 inch
- 2 teaspoons chili powder
- 1 tablespoon olive oil
- Juice of 1 lime
- 1 teaspoon onion powder
- 1 bell pepper red, cut into pieces of 1 inch
- 2 teaspoons olive oil
- 1 bell pepper yellow, cut into pieces of 1 inch
- 2 teaspoons garlic powder
- ½ red onion, cut into pieces of 1 inch

Instructions:

Toss in lime juice, olive oil, spices, and pork cubes in a big zipped bag. Mix well.

Marinate for half an hour or overnight if possible.

Soak your skewers in water if they are wooden.

Thread the pork pieces, bell peppers then onions alternatively on the skewers.

Turn the grill on and put the kebabs onto the grill. Also, drizzle using olive oil to prevent any sticking.

Cook the kebabs for 4 minutes from each side and until there are light marks of grill on them.

Recipe 27 - Chicken Veggie Fajitas

This recipe is one of the pleasant chicken Veggie fajitas recipes that will satisfy your taste buds.

Serving size: 4 servings

Total time: 20 minutes

Ingredients:

- 4 warmed flour tortillas of 6 inches
- 3 tablespoons lemon juice
- 2 teaspoons canola oil
- 1 garlic clove, minced
- ½ teaspoon ground cumin
- 1 tablespoon soy sauce
- ½ teaspoon dried oregano
- ¾ lb. boneless and skinless chicken breasts, cut into strips of ½ inch
- 1 tablespoon Worchester sauce
- 1 onion small, sliced, separated into rings
- ½ each sweet red, green, and yellow pepper medium, julienned
- cheddar cheese Shredded, optional

Instructions:

In a small bowl, combine the marinade ingredients (ingredients except for cheese, vegetables, chicken, and lemon juice mixture). Place chicken and vegetables in a single layer in a greased 15x10x1-in. baking pan drizzle with 1/4 cup lemon juice mixture.

Broil 4-6 in. from the heat for 4 minutes.

Turn chicken and vegetable drizzle with the remaining lemon juice mixture. Broil 4 minutes longer or until chicken juices run clear.

Serve on tortillas, with cheese if desired.

Recipe 28 - Pronto Chicken Fajitas:

Try this amazing pronto chicken fajitas recipe and thank me later.

Serving size: 5 servings

Total time: 10 minutes

Ingredients:

- 1 package of 14 ounces pepper strips frozen, thawed
- ½ teaspoon salt
- 1 onion medium, halved, sliced
- 2 packages of 6 ounces each southwestern chicken strips ready-to-use
- 1 tablespoon canola oil
- 5 warmed flour tortillas of 8 inches
- 1 teaspoon fresh cilantro minced
- ½ teaspoon garlic powder
- ¼ teaspoon pepper
- Optional toppings: cheddar cheese shredded, guacamole, sour cream, and salsa

Instructions:

In a large skillet, sauté pepper strips and onions in oil until tender.

Add the chicken strips, cilantro, salt, garlic powder, and pepper heat through.

Spoon onto tortillas fold them on the sides. Serve with toppings of your choice.

Recipe 29 - Chicken Fajita pizza:

Try this delicious chicken fajita pizza recipe and serve your loved ones.

Serving size: 6 servings

Total time: 35 minutes

Ingredients:

- 1 package of ¼ ounces dry yeast active
- 2 teaspoons divided salt
- 1 teaspoon sugar
- 1 teaspoon garlic powder
- 2 ½ cups flour all-purpose
- 1 lb. cut into strips boneless and skinless chicken breasts
- 2 cups onions sliced
- 4 tablespoons divided canola oil
- 1 cup salsa
- 1 cup warm water (115F)
- 2 cups Monterrey Jack shredded or mozzarella cheese part-skim shredded
- 2 teaspoons chili powder
- 2 cups green peppers sliced

Instructions:

Take a large mixing bowl, then mix yeast and water. Include flour, two tablespoons of oil, sugar, and 1 tsp salt.

Beat the mixture by hand for about 20 strokes. Now cover. Let it rest for 15 minutes.

Divide the dough in half and press each into the pizza pan of 12 inches. Now prick it using a fork multiple times. Bake for 8 minutes at 425 F.

Sauté the chicken in the rest of the oil using a skillet. Add the remaining salt, garlic powder, chili powder, peppers, and onions, and cook until the vegetables become tender.

Spoon the mixture on the crusts and top with cheese and salsa. Bake these for 15 to 18 minutes.

Recipe 30 - Wasabi Beef Fajitas:

Give this delicious Wasabi Beef fajitas recipe, and you will get to crave more.

Serving size: 8 servings

Total time: 20 minutes

Ingredients:

- 12 onions along with tops (green), cut lengthwise in half
- 2 teaspoons cornstarch
- 2 teaspoons fresh ginger root minced
- 1 minced garlic clove
- 2 tablespoons divided sesame oil
- 3 tablespoons soy sauce reduced-sodium
- 1 lb. beef stir-fry uncooked strips
- 2 teaspoons prepared wasabi
- 1 cup coleslaw mix
- 1 large julienned red pepper sweet
- 8 warmed flour tortillas of 8 inches

Instructions:

Mix garlic, ginger, wasabi, soy, and cornstarch in a bowl until blended.

Heat oil 1 tbsp on medium heat in a skillet.

Add the beef and stir fry for 5 minutes and remove it from the pan.

Stir-fry red pepper and green onions for 3 minutes and stir in the cornstarch mixture.

Bring the mixture to boiling and cook for a minute or two while stirring. Heat thoroughly.

Serve with coleslaw mix and tortillas.

Conclusion

This book is designed to give you very unique and interesting fajita recipes full of different tastes. The recipes are guaranteed to make you happy. These are good recipes not only because it gives us a nice taste but are easy to prepare and you can enjoy with friends and family by throwing fajita parties. No one ever says I don't like a fajita, so these will be very well-liked by people around you.

About the Author

Since he was a child, Logan King enjoyed watching his mom cook. For him, it was even more fun than playing with his friends. That's how he fell in love with cooking. In fact, the first thing he ever cooked on his own was a cupcake, a surprise for his little sister, which not even his mom was expecting.

Now, supported by the whole family he is constantly sharing new recipes of his own creations. He finished a gastronomy academy when he was 18 and continued his career as a chef and recipe developer.

Now his goal is to educate and help people fell in love with cooking as he did. Actually, he is advising mothers and fathers to give their children an opportunity in the kitchen, because they never know, maybe their kid could be the next top chef.

Even though he pursued a career as a chef, his cookbooks are designed for everyone, with and without cooking experience. He even says, "even if you don't know where your knife is you will be able to do my recipes."

The gastronomy field is large and there is no end in the options, ingredient combinations, and cooking techniques. That's why he tries his best to keep his audience informed about the newest recipes, and even give them a chance to modify his recipes so that they can find a new one, one that they can call their own.

Appendices

I am not stopping with this book. There are going to a lot more so make sure you are ready for the amazing recipes that you will be able to get from me. You can always be sure that they are going to be simple and easy to follow.

But thank you for choosing my book. I know that you haven't made a mistake and you will realize that too, well, as soon as you start making the recipes.

Please do share your experience about the written as well as the practical part of this book. Leave feedback that will help me and other people, I'll greatly apricate this.

Thank you once more

Have a great adventure with my book

Yours Truly

Logan King

Printed in Great Britain
by Amazon